KU-414-889

A HUNDRED DOORS

BY THE SAME AUTHOR

POETRY

No Continuing City
An Exploded View
Man Lying on a Wall
The Echo Gate
Poems 1963–1983
Gorse Fires
The Ghost Orchid
Selected Poems
The Weather in Japan
Snow Water
Collected Poems

AUTOBIOGRAPHY

Tuppenny Stung

AS EDITOR

Causeway: The Arts in Ulster
Under the Moon, Over the Stars: Children's Poetry
Further Reminiscences: Paul Henry
Selected Poems: Louis MacNeice
Poems: Louis MacNeice
Poems: W. R. Rodgers
Selected Poems: John Hewitt (with Frank Ormsby)
20th Century Irish Poems

A HUNDRED DOORS

Michael Longley

CAPE POETRY

Published by Jonathan Cape 2011

2 4 6 8 10 9 7 5 3

Copyright © Michael Longley 2011

Michael Longley has asserted his right under the Copyright, Designs
and Patents Act 1988 to be identified as the author of this work

This book is sold subject to the condition that it shall not,
by way of trade or otherwise, be lent, resold, hired out,
or otherwise circulated without the publisher's prior
consent in any form of binding or cover other than that
in which it is published and without a similar condition,
including this condition, being imposed
on the subsequent purchaser.

First published in Great Britain in 2011 by
Jonathan Cape
Random House, 20 Vauxhall Bridge Road,
London SW1V 2SA

www.rbooks.co.uk

Addresses for companies within The Random House Group Limited can be found at:
www.randomhouse.co.uk/offices.htm

The Random House Group Limited Reg. No. 954009

A CIP catalogue record for this book
is available from the British Library

ISBN 9780224091381
ISBN 9780224093781 (Leather-bound Limited Edition)

The Random House Group Limited supports The Forest Stewardship Council (FSC),
the leading international forest certification organisation. All our titles that are
printed on Greenpeace approved FSC certified paper carry the FSC logo.
Our paper procurement policy can be found at:
www.rbooks.co.uk/environment

Typeset in Bembo by Palimpsest Book Production Limited,
Falkirk, Stirlingshire
Printed and bound in Great Britain by
MPG Books Ltd, Bodmin, Cornwall

For Frank Ormsby

We are sitting beneath stained-glass windows
In our snug in The Crown, sipping our pints,
Taking confession from our reflections
Among flowers painted on the mirrors.

TOWER HAMLETS LIBRARIES	
91000000725580	
Bertrams	05/08/2011
AN	£10.00
THISCA	TH11000625

CONTENTS

The future writ in white spaces
Barbara Guest

CALL

Alone at Carrigskeewaun for the millennium
My friend sits at the hearth keeping the cottage warm.
Is it too late to phone him? Is it midnight yet?
That could be me, a meadow pipit calling out.
Otters are crossing from Dooaghtry to Corragaun.
There are mallards and widgeon and teal for him to count.
Three dolphins are passing the Carricknashinnagh shoal.
He has kept for this evening firewood that is very old.
Bog deal's five thousand years make the room too hot.
How snugly the meadow pipit fits the merlin's foot.

MARSH CINQUEFOIL

Unanticipated here
In this Mayo boreen,
It brings back her long
Hair and her laughter
As she shares the Irish
For flowers, for the chough
Closing its red toes
Above our heads twenty
Years ago in windy
Macha na Bó, marsh
Cinquefoil, the purple
Sultry out-of-the-way
Entangled bog-berry,
Her favourite flower.

HORSESHOE

I find a rusty horseshoe where skylarks
Rise from the sheepshitty path, God-sparks,
Sound-glints for bridle and bridle hand.
I am the farrier in this townland.

OTTER CUBS

As I listened to their gasps and sneezes,
They reappeared in memory out there
Among the reeds, and at my feet milkwort's
Sapphire glimmers seemed retina-born.

THE NEW WINDOW

Sitting up in bed with binoculars I scan
My final resting place at Dooaghtry
Through the new window, soul-space
For my promontory, high and dry, Fairy
Fort the children called it, rising above
Otter-rumours and, now, the swans' nest
Among yellow flags, a blur of bog cotton,
Afterfeathers from a thousand preenings.

AT DAWN

Wakened from a grandfatherly nightmare
I sleepwalked around the cottage at dawn,
Checking windows and wind-rattled gates.
The westerly blew me wren-song, then
Wing-music. Five swans creaking towards
Corragaun Lake would have been enough.
I have to imagine the sixth swan
That was definitely there at the zenith.

THE LEVERET
for my grandson, Benjamin

This is your first night in Carrigskeewaun.
The Owennadornaun is so full of rain
You arrived in Paddy Morrison's tractor,
A bumpy approach in your father's arms
To the cottage where, all of one year ago,
You were conceived, a fire-seed in the hearth.
Did you hear the wind in the fluffy chimney?
Do you hear the wind tonight, and the rain
And a shore bird calling from the mussel reefs?
Tomorrow I'll introduce you to the sea,
Little hoplite. Have you been missing it?
I'll park your chariot by the otters' rock
And carry you over seaweed to the sea.
There's a tufted duck on David's lake
With her sootfall of hatchlings, pompoms
A day old and already learning to dive.
We may meet the stoat near the erratic
Boulder, a shrew in his mouth, or the merlin
Meadow-pipit-hunting. But don't be afraid.
The leveret breakfasts under the fuchsia
Every morning, and we shall be watching.
I have picked wild flowers for you, scabious
And centaury in a jam-jar of water
That will bend and magnify the daylight.
This is your first night in Carrigskeewaun.

CHRISTMAS TREE
for Jacob

You are my second grandson, Christmas-born.
I put on specs to read your face. Whispering
Sweet nothings to your glistening eyelids,
Am I outspoken compared with you? You sleep
While I carry you to our elderly beech.
Your forefinger twitches inside its mitten.
Do you feel at home in my aching crook?
There will be room beneath your fontanel
For this branchy diagram of winter.
I take you back indoors to the Christmas tree.
Dangling for you among the fairy lights
Are the zodiac's animals and people.

THE WREN

I am writing too much about Carrigskeewaun,
I think, until you two come along, my grandsons,
And we generalise at once about cows and sheep.
A day here represents a life-time, bird's-foot trefoil
Among wild thyme, dawn and dusk muddled on the ground,
The crescent moon fading above Mweelrea's shoulder
As hares sip brackish water at the stepping stones
And the innovative raven flips upside down
As though for you.
                                    I burble under your siesta
Like a contrapuntal runnel, and the heather
Stand that shelters the lesser twayblade shelters you.
We sleepwalk around a townland whooper swans
From the tundra remember, and the Saharan
Wheatear. I want you both to remember me
And what the wind-tousled wren has been saying
All day long from fence posts and the fuchsia depths,
A brain-rattling bramble-song inside a knothole.

LULLABY
for Eddie

The vixen will hear you cry, and the swans
On their eggless experimental nest,
And the insomniac curlew, and the leveret
That leaves a dew-path across the lawn.

HEDGE-JUG

Cocooning us in their whisper of contact-
Calls as I carry you into the house, seven
Or six long-tailed tits flitter out of the hedge.
How can there be enough love to go round,
Conor Michael, grandson number four?
The tits build a dome with wool and moss and
Spiders' webs and feathers, then camouflage
With many lichen fragments their hedge-jug,
Feather-poke that grows as the fledglings grow.

A GARLAND
for Catherine

I've been thinking about you for a long time
In faraway places like Piso Livadi
Where on May Day they festoon with wild
Flowers the masts of their fishing smacks.

The morning you were born I wrote a poem
About the Shetlands. After four grandsons
I was half-expecting you, Catherine:
The oystercatcher's peep, the harbour seal.

THE FOLD

Why would the ewes and their lambs
Assemble as though hypnotised
Around the cottage? Do they sense
A storm on its way? Or a fox?
Darkness and quiet are folding
All the sheep of Carrigskeewaun,
Their fleeces lustrous, long wool
For a baby's comfort-blanket,
For Catherine asleep in her crib
This midnight, our lambing-time.

THE SIXTH SWAN

You are the sixth swan, Maisie:
The other five have flown
To the vanishing lake
And wait beyond the ridge
For you: but stay a while
In my mind, dawn-memory,
Little zenith-lingerer.

A SWAN'S EGG

Handling this century-old
Alabaster emptiness,
I shadow the nest robber
Who blew the white and yolk
Of a cygnet waiting before
The Great War to follow cob
And pen across Glen Lough;
Who wrote around the black hole
Collector's particulars
That sit in a cabinet
Brimming with bird silences,
Feathery non-existences,
A swan's egg among wren
Pearls and kingfisher pearls.

On the Shetlands we don't know anyone,
So we gossip about the animals
Or we contact home on the mobile.
As we wait at Toft for the Yell ferry
You walk up and down the little beach
Too deep in conversation and sad news
To notice an otter's kelp-flashes. Look!
I'm trying not to frighten him away.

You climb alone to where witches burned
And disturb a white hare. Albino
Or snowy-coated still? I've no idea.
Shy behind his streaming forelock, he
Approaches us, one dishevelled pony,
A grandchild's mount. Shall I comb his mane?
His hoof-prints fill with rain and inspire me,
My hobbling, diminutive Pegasus.

WHALSAY

He fitted all of the island
Inside a fisherman's float — his
Cosmology of sea breezes
Cooling the seabirds' eggs
Or filling otter prints with sand:

For such phenomena, for
Sea lavender and spindrift, he —
Ravenous, insomniac — beach-
Combed the exact dialect words
Under a sky of green glass.

SHETLAND MOUSE-EAR

We got as far as Unst,
No nearer, as if the idea
Of Shetland mouse-ear's white
Petals, hairy leaves, roots
In debris, growing nowhere else
In the world was enough.

PRELUDE

I heard in my inner ear
At the Broch of Gurness
Bach – that childlike first prelude
Clear as a rock pool, perfect
Pitch, barnacles on kelp.
Whoever was playing sat
Painfully on his stone chair
For hours on end so that
As well as oystercatcher
And curlew – penny-whistlers
From other musical sites
Beyond the wind – the stone
That bruised his perineum
Was part of the prelude.

THE CARTS
Poem Beginning with a Line of Yannis Ritsos

Outside passed the carts and the moon
And the moon and its reflection
Made a cart track for nameless souls
Across the lake without a name.

A HUNDRED DOORS

God! I'm lighting candles again, still
The sentimental atheist, family
Names a kind of prayer or poem, my muse
Our Lady of a Hundred Doors.

Supervised by a xenophobic
Sacristan, I plant in dusty sand
Names and faces that follow me
As far as windows in the floor:

Marble stumps aching through glass
For their pagan temple, the warm
Inwardness Praxiteles brought out,
The intelligence of stone.

The sacristan who picks my flame-
Flowers and blows them out, only minutes
Old, knows I am watching and he
Doesn't care as he shortens my lives.

BEE ORCHID

We returned to the Byzantine path's
Camomile-strewn marble pavement
And dusty oregano to look again,
Before the snails, for the bee orchid.

Pollineum like a brain, the brainy
Bumble-bee disguise. On our knees
Among wild garlic, almost at prayer,
We forgot about adder and lizard,

And nearly missed in a juniper
The blackcap's jet black. We waited
And waited for his connoisseur's
Restrained aria among the prickles.

TWAYBLADE

Twayblade. We find it together,
The two of us, inconspicuous
With greeny petals in long grass,
Lips forked like a man, two leaves
Some call sweethearts, our plant today,
Fed on snowmelt and wood shadows.

PUFF-BALL

When we picked mushrooms at midnight
Among intersecting fairy rings,
You said moonlight had ripened them.

Later I found the moon's image –
The full moon's – a giant puff-ball
Taking shape as in a low cloud.

CLOUDBERRIES

You give me cloudberry jam from Lapland,
Bog amber, snow-line titbits, scrumptious
Cloudberries sweetened slowly by the cold,
And costly enough for cloudberry wars
(Diplomatic wars, my dear).
                              Imagine us
Among the harvesters, keeping our distance
In sphagnum fields on the longest day
When dawn and dusk like frustrated lovers
Can kiss, legend has it, once a year. Ah,
Kisses at our age, cloudberry kisses.

JANUARY

The townland is growing older too.
It makes sense to be here in the cold:
Fuchsia's flowerless carmine, willow's
Purple besom. We are lovers still.
Mistiness and half a moon provide
Our soul-arena, a tawny ring.

MARS

Mars was as close as this so long ago
It reminded us of the Neanderthals.
We were stargazing under a beech tree
That could have sheltered United Irishmen.
We were squinting at Mars through binoculars.
'The tree is getting closer to the house.'
'I hope it touches the house before it dies.'
'I hope it touches the house before we die.'

FOXGLOVES

Rebecca, our first-born, now thirty-nine,
Flies in to check that I am well again
And spots beside the bed the photograph
I took of you when you were carrying her,
Six months gone in your purple polo-neck
And blue smock, and laughing, I remember,
Because I have decorated with sea pinks
Your black abundant hair, and given you
Foxgloves to hold as though to welcome her
To the strand at Inch and the Kerry hills.
Can you go on smiling from your dune-throne
With your hair and hands full of summer flowers?
Because the marram grass is damp and sandy
I have spread a yellow oilskin under you.

THE LIFEBOAT

I have imagined an ideal death in Charlie Gaffney's
Pub in Louisburgh: he pulls me the pluperfect pint
As I, at the end of the bar next the charity boxes,
Expire on my stool, head in hand, without a murmur.

I have just helped him to solve his crossword puzzle
And we commune with ancestral photos in the alcove.
He doesn't notice that I am dead until closing time
And he sweeps around my feet.
                          But it's Charlie Gaffney
Who has died. Charlie, how do I buy a fishing licence?
Shall I let the dog out? Would the fire take another sod?
The pub might as well be empty forever now. I launch
The toy lifeboat at my elbow with an old penny.

LENA

    The first person I didn't want to die
    Was Lena Hardy, the 'country girl'
    Who during the war took care of me.
    She didn't die. She went away. Lena.

    I can remember where I haven't been:
    A townland that overlooks a lake.
    We are strolling across the Wee Homes.
    We are trying to find the Beggars' Bush.

MARY O'TOOLE

Imagine Mary O'Toole
Of Inishdeigil hoisting
The turf fire in a pot when
Spring tides flooded the hearth,

Dropping a willow-pattern
Shard at Rough Creek that shone
Under the waves, then
Leaving her tiny island.

At Carrigskeewaun she said
'Now I can walk anywhere'
And wandered between
Two sandy-bottomed lakes.

Imagine Mary O'Toole
And me coinciding and
Walking through the white gate
To all of the islands.

THE HOLLY BUSH
in memory of Dorothy Molloy

Frosty Carrigskeewaun. I am breaking ice
Along the salt marsh's soggy margins
And scaring fieldfares out of the holly bush
And redwings, their consorts, chestnut-brown
Flashing one way, chestnut-red another,
Fragments of the January dawn-light
That Killary focuses on the islands
Before it clears the shoulder of Mweelrea.
Caher Island and Inishturk are frosty too.
In the short-lived spotlight they look like cut-
Outs and radiate apricot from within.
I learn of your death in this weather and
Of your book arriving the day after,
Your first and last slim volume. Dorothy,
You read your poems just once and I was there.
The poets you loved are your consorts now.
Golden plovers – a hundred or more – turn
And give back dawn-light from their undersides.
The edge of the dunes wears a fiery fringe.

GARDENING IN CARDOSO

Wild flowers become weeds
In this small triangular
Garfagnana garden
Where I uproot herb robert,
Spurge, wall-devouring
Valerian, garlicky
Ramsons, dead nettles.
What about oregano
No higher than dogs' piss,
And pennywort protecting
The lizard's hideaway?
I cut back the wild fig tree,
Its roots under the *casa*
Squeezing our waterpipes,
Dozy snails its only fruit.
From acacia – beeless,
Unrelieved – a sexual
Heaviness marries me
And five old women – last
In the village to chant
The Whitsun rosary next
Door at San Rocco's shrine.
I leave them shepherd's purse's
Seed pods – little hearts –
Spoon-shaped petals on spikes.

FIREWOOD

Out of the darkness and
Up the spiral staircase
I am carrying logs,
An armful every day,
Firewood for winter when
I shall not be here – wild
Fig perhaps – white sap
For curing warts, scrotum-
Concealing leaves – blackthorn,
Chestnut – for all I know –
From the skinny waterfall,
Antique olive branches,
Sycamore, mulberry –
At the back of the wood pile
Underneath the *casa*
Logs that will never burn
Disintegrating year
By year, forgetfulness,
Woodlouse, scorpion.

TONGUE ORCHID

I pass the first dilapidated
Chestnut that holds in its leaves
The waterfall's hurlygush,
When you call me back
Through tangles of paradise
Lily, bastard balm,
Nightshade, vetch to our very
First wasp-seducing
Tongue orchid, brownish red
Napkins neatly folded
As for a love-feast:
Why can't we find a name
For purple candelabra
And dusk-stars like signals
To amorous fireflies, yet
So white in their thicket
They mark the path ending
And things coming to an end?

MISSING MARIE

Missing you involves
Hilltop orchids
High above the house,
And a pipistrelle
Down beside the vines,
A hole in its wing
The size of the moon
When I pick it up,
A fuzzy hunchback
With chattering teeth.
The orchids withdraw
To purple shadow
And escape their name.
Darkness is pouring
Through the bat's hopeless
Veiny membrane.

FLOWER-PIECE

Robert Schumann's *Blumenstück*,
The last music you listened to:
Mood-swings, campanula, wood
Anemones, your flower-piece.

PAMELA

In your window winter-flowering jasmine's
Reflections frame the music you practised
Before you died. Intermezzi. December's
Yellow flowers. Sorrow's cradlesong.

SISTER AGNES

We walk away from Woodtown
Abbott Farm full of relations –
Along the lane the creamery
Tanker makes pot-holey
Muddying rosehip and haw
But not these black lights – field
Mouse eyes in privet – privet
Berries or elderberries –
And listen to rook politics
In the last beech leaves before
We go back to celebrate
A long-dead nun – Sister Agnes –
Your cousin how many times
Removed – poultry expert
And Mother Superior –
Who once bathed – imagine – your
Mathematical father – soon
To leave her in the dark
And bump down the lane – the Plough
Juddering this way and that
And filling our windscreen.

ENCOUNTERS

I

The dog-collar approaching me
Just after the war – between
Pickie Pool and Miss Good's
Guest house – would save my soul –
But I tore up his tracts and
Buried them in grubby sand
As soon as he'd departed
With his embarrassing god.

II

'Want to learn the half-nelson?
Cry out when it hurts.' Oh dear,
Did he rub up against me?
How close was I to death
Behind shadowy willows?
I burst into tears, then raced
Along the Lagan towpath
On my Hercules bike.

III

'Do you mind my hand on your – ?'
'No,' I said, eager to please,
Then slipped away in darkness
And hid among empty seats
And watched him disappear
Forever into the Gents.

Shivering in black woolly trunks
At Pickie Pool, how could I make
Even smaller my sex-bump?
In the men's changing area
Not everyone was so modest.
A show-off performed nude hand-
Stands against the whitewashed wall.
He comes back in miniature
A lifetime later when I see
How neatly flop a sleepy
Pipistrelle's genitals – sex
Berries high in the branches.

THE POKER
in memory of Sam Thompson

When I was studying Greek and Latin,
College-bound, my twin, apprenticed
At the Yard, was turning on his lathe
The brass handle for this poker – cast
Iron twist and forged tip – sweated on –
Old-fashioned brazing. Shall I poke the fire?

Shipwright, playwright and trade unionist,
Old Decency's philosopher, our own
Diogenes – though not a cynic –
You growled at lickspittles and toadies
And opened a way over the bridge
For Jews and gypsies, all refugees,

Persons displaced by our bigoted
Hometown. Can you hear them in the gods
Clapping and cheering your curtain call?
There's a Brasso bottle in my toolkit.
Shall I polish my brother's poker?
It's precious, Sam. It belongs to you.

THE SIGNAL BOX AT DUNDALK
for Terence Brown

On the homeward journey north
I hear your husky staccato
Celebrate north County Dublin's
Little harbours with their laid-up
Recuperating red smacks.

They remind me of you, Northern
Dubliner, along with that gravelly
Causeway, migratory geese
To the left, on the right dapper
Shelduck, rain-foretelling plovers.

There are three horses in a field,
A winter-pruned apple orchard
And a walled garden in ruins.
Am I making this all up? No.
At Dundalk you leave the train.

I think I can make you out,
Terence, behind steamy glass
In the old signal box, precise,
Knowledgable, pulling levers
And bringing order to the lines.

A GUST
for Eddie Linden at 70

I'm thinking of the pope and you, Eddie,
As I dander towards the New York Public
Library to peek at the field note-books
Of Edward Thomas wandering in England
In pursuit of spring before poetry and war.
Somewhere between Dorval and La Guardia
I encountered John Paul among the clouds
Like a surge of energy from the engines.
Now he lies stiff and full of chemicals
In precarious white hat and purple slippers
Saying the rosary over and over.
It all depends on the embalmer's craft.
The Poles cry out for his leathery heart.
John Paul was *musarum sacerdos* (part-time)
And you, Eddie, are a priest of the muses too
(Aquarian Order), your Vatican City
All the practitioners, the bad and good.
A shell blast killed Edward Thomas, a gust
That still riffles the pages in the library
On this bright popeless early April day.
Through the Door of the Sacraments I follow
John Paul and Edward and Eddie Linden.

He has pissed himself. Is he high or ill?
He swings towards me on a single crutch
And smells of the sympathetic hyacinths
Sent from Rotterdam which Hitler flattened.
Kerouac's crutches are kept in the Berg.
Is not this the greatest of institutions
With levels we both know nothing about?
We take the elevator past the top floor
To the imaginary roof-garden.

FOOTNOTE

I deciphered his handwriting for Edna
In the Berg Collection, and helped them both
To rise above the table-top's green baize
When Edward 'grasped the stile by the holly.'

VISITING STANLEY KUNITZ

I have flown the Atlantic
To reach you in your chair.
Cuddling up, we talk about
Flowers, important things,
And hold hands to celebrate
Spring gentian's heavenly
(Strictly speaking) blue.
You grow anemones,
You say, wind's daughters.
I say the world should name
A flower after you, Stanley.
We read each other poems.
You who'll be a hundred soon
Take forever to sign
My copy of *Passing Through*.
What flower can I offer you
From Ireland? Bog asphodel
Is the colour of your shirt.
Grass of Parnassus? Mountain
Everlasting in New York?
Your zimmer-gavotte suggests
Madder with its goose-grassy
Tenacity, your age-spots
Winter-flowering mudwort.
But no, no. Let it be
Spring gentian, summer sky
At sunset, Athene's eyes,
Five petals, earthbound star.

ONCE
for Maurice Harmon

You've only to do it once,
Write a poem, I mean, one poem
As good as the elegy
For himself that Chidiock
Tichborne jotted down
The night before the gallows,
Castration, disembowelment,
A smile on his face, surely,
As he found the syllables
And the breathing spaces.

GUNNER LONGLEY

My namesake, accident-prone
Amid detonators and
Powder-bags, ill at ease
In the cordite-risky gun
Turret, Gunner Longley,
We meet in this windy field,
Saxons among Viking ghosts,
My wealden-distant cousin
Buried on Hoy. That curlew
Might as well be piping you
On board, and that stonechat
Calling you like a bugler
To sea-spray assembly
On the sea-rinsed *Collingwood*.

BUMF

I

There was no bumf for Tommies
In the shithouse – death's
Cul-de-sac – excrement's grave –
Squatting – a sniper's target –
Nothing to wipe your arse with
Except letters from home –
Love letters – ink and skidmarks –
Radiant blue and shit –
And there was no grass either.

II

Who would empty the buckets?
Those who were about to die
In No Man's Land envied
The long-lived shit-wallahs.

CITATION

It is like a poem. It is better than a poem,
The citation for my father's Military Cross
Dividing itself up into lines like this: 'For
Conspicuous gallantry and devotion to duty
In leading the waves of his company in a raid
And being the first to enter both objectives
In spite of a severe shrapnel wound in the thigh.
After killing several of the enemy himself,
He directed the fire of his Lewis gunners
And rifle bombers on to a working party
Of over 100 of the enemy, and controlled
The mopping-up of the enemy dug-outs.'
Kept alive by his war cry and momentum,
I shiver behind him on the fire-step.

HIGH WOOD

My father is good at mopping up:
Steam rises from the blood and urine.

VOLUNTEER

The old gamekeeper could recall a young groundsman
Leaving Ballynahinch to cycle to Galway
And on to the Western Front, his red
Neckerchief like a necklace of poppies.

TRENCH FOOT

Christ is washing the feet of his Company.
He has an endless supply of talcum
And old newspapers for lining their boots.
He is promoted after Passchendaele.

VIMY RIDGE

From a forward observation post the day
Before he is killed he writes to his wife:
'Between the terrific noise of the guns I
Can hear two hedge sparrows making love.'

INTO BATTLE

The Hampshires march into battle with bare knees.
Full of shrapnel holes are the leaves on the trees.

WOODEN SAILS

The ship of the fens is Ely Cathedral, its wooden
Sails becalmed below-decks like a gigantic ledger
Crammed with the names of unremembered soldiers
Under their villages' names – Shudy Camps, Little
Chishill, Abbingdon Piggots, Prick Willow, Swaffam
Bulbeck – until the sails billow with our lamentations
And the ship of the fens sets sail over the fens
To Fen Drayton, Ponders Bridge, Tadlow, Elm, Ely.

OLD SOLDIERS

We are both old soldiers now, my father and I.
Socrates stalking the battlefield at Delion
Held his ground. Idomeneus in the *Iliad*
Could still hurl his lethal spear and retrieve it,

But only just. King Priam who loved his dogs
As my father his red setters and spaniels,
Dreaded them chewing at his pathetic corpse's
White head and white beard and bleeding genitals.

ALTARPIECE

The page-boy in the bottom right-hand corner
Looks out and draws me into the diagonal
Drama. Or so I thought. Rather, he brings
Histrionic saint and successful soldier
(A Titian self-portrait?) down to my level.

I'm distracted already by the German bomb
Displayed on the wall next to the painting.
It pierced in February nineteen-eighteen
The basilica roof but failed to explode,
A girl's breast falling still, a rusty teardrop.

The page-boy catches my eye before I go.
Buskers are serenading Mother and Child.
We need more angels, cloud-treaders, cherubic
Instrumentalists, bomb-disposal experts.
The sky is a minefield. We shall all get hurt.

CYGNUS

Cygnus infuriates Achilles who just cannot kill him –
Spears bouncing off each shoulder as off a stone wall
Or cliff face, that cumbersome body blunting his sword. So,
He pummels chin and temples – knock-out punches – and
Trips him up and kneels on ribcage and adam's apple
And thrapples Cygnus's windpipe with his helmet-thongs.

But this is no triumph for Achilles: he has strangled
Neptune's son who grows webs at once between his fingers
While his hair turns snowy and feathery and his neck
Lengthens and curves out from a downy chest and his lips
Protrude as a knobbly beak through which he wheezes
And he is transformed into a – yes (hence the name) –

A white swan that flies above the bloody battlefield.

HELEN

It is snowing, Helen. You want to go.
Your ashes fall like snow. Now at last
Those terrible numbers above your wrist
Add up to you. Your ashes fall like snow.

HAWTHORN

Unsuperstitiously I snapped a hawthorn sprig
And kept it alive in a mug of tap water,
For it reminded me of one of his sentences,
Bud clusters, the makings of snow in May,
October sunshine, and a blaze of hardhearted
Haws on the original Aughawillan hedge.

CLOUD ORCHID
in memory of Raymond Piper

Ours was a language of flowers,
As Christopher Smart would have it:
An Antrim meadow, unimproved,
Covered in lady's smock and ragged
Robin; pink pyramids at Killard;
The colours of the Union Flag
In the Republic – gentian,
Avens, cranesbill – our Ulster joke;
Spring gentian's ultimate blue
The secret of the cosmos, close
To the ground among the grasses.

You are standing and pointing, first
At the cheeky Sheela-na-gig,
Then at her offspring – unexpected
Bee orchids – around her doorway
In Kilnaboy; near Lough Bunny
Like an antique flasher in the wind
Spreading your overcoat to screen
A frantic dropwort; after
Our solitary fly orchid,
Conjuring on a bridge for me
Clouds of orange-tipped butterflies.

Undistracted in your greenhouse-
Studio by caterpillar
Droppings from the mimosa tree
That twisted overhead, you
Gazed up through the branches and
The broken pane imagining
Your last flower portrait – 'for flowers

Are good both for the living
And the dead' – the minuscule
Cloud Orchid that grows in the rain
Forest's misty canopy.

The rusty fuse you brought home
From a specific hummock
In Carrigskeewaun – autumn
Lady's-tresses – yet to flower
Under your greenhouse's moony
Glass in Belfast – do you want
Me to move it from the sill
Onto the ground for moisture
Or re-pot it or hire, as once
We did, *Mystical Rose*
And chug out to the Saltees?

WHITE FARMHOUSE

Colin Middleton knew that he was dying
And fitted all the colours he had ever used
Into his last painting, a white farmhouse
Among drumlins, the gable and chimneys
White, the corn harvested by his palette-knife,
A besmirching of corn poppy, cornflower,
One blue-black spinney, triangles of sunlight
Disappearing between Octobery hedges,
Another farmhouse in the distance like home.
Colin Middleton was a friend of mine
When I was young. How can I count the colours?
There are no doors or windows in the building,
No outhouses. I name the picture for myself.
Titles, said Duchamp, are invisible colours.

A MOBILE FOR MAISIE

Out of old parcel-string, a spool, safety
Pins, cotton wool, clothes pegs, tartan scraps
(Your father sews kilts in the next room)
Your mother who has painted the shutters
With foxgloves, bluebells, water-lilies,
Bumble bees and a dragonfly, and strung
Fairy lights along the mantelpiece, now
In the small hours makes you a mobile,
Her lonesome, sleepy improvisation,
Matter-of-fact rosary for your crib, a
Carrick-a-Rede bridge that stretches far back
(Your great-grandfather, my father, wore
A kilt in the Great War) and home again.
She will suckle you. Can you smell her milk?

PROOFS

I have locked overnight in my antique Peugeot
At the channel, close to stepping stones, the proofs,
Uncorrected, of my fifty years of poetry. What
Would I add to the inventory? A razor shell,
A mermaid's purse, some relic of this windless
Sea-roar-surrounded February quietude?

GREENSHANK

When I've left Carrigskeewaun for the last time,
I hope you discover something I've overlooked,
Greenshanks, say, two or three, elegantly probing
Where sand from the white strand and the burial mound
Blows in. How long will Corragaun remain a lake?
If I had to choose a bird call for reminding you,
The greenshank's estuarial fluting would do.

NOTES & ACKNOWLEDGEMENTS

'The Leveret' and 'The Wren' made an earlier appearance as the epilogue to my *Collected Poems* (2006).

Despite sounding urban, the Hiberno-English word *townland* (pp. 2, 7, 18, 20) is usually rural. Townlands, to quote my friend the late Brendan Adams, 'vary in size from a few acres to several thousand acres, but the very large ones are confined to mountain moorland. Each townland has its name and defined boundaries, so there is no spot in Ireland without a name . . .' (*Nomina 2*: 1978). There is only one cottage in the townland of Carrigskeewaun.

The great Scottish poet Hugh MacDiarmid lived on the Shetland island of Whalsay from 1933 to 1942.

'Mary O'Toole' and 'Firewood' were included in *Many Mansions*, a limited edition published by the Stoney Gate Press on behalf of the Trustees of the Ireland Chair of Poetry in 2009. 'The Poker' was commissioned by Martin Lynch and Green Shoot Productions to mark the fiftieth anniversary revival in 2010 of *Over the Bridge*, Sam Thompson's play about sectarianism in the Belfast Shipyard. It was printed in the theatre programme.

Dorothy Molloy's first collection *Hare Soup* was published in 2004. When I wrote 'The Holly Bush' I was not to know that two posthumous collections of her work would eventually appear.

'A Gust' was written for an edition of *Aquarius* that celebrated Eddie Linden's seventieth birthday. 'Once' was included in *Honouring the Word*, a festschrift published by Salmon Press in celebration of Maurice Harmon's eightieth birthday. 'The Signal Box at Dundalk' was written for *Twelve by Two for Terence*, a tribute to Terence Brown, edited by Nicholas Grene and published by the English Department of Trinity College Dublin.

The citation for my father's Military Cross was published in *The Times* on 27 April 1918. He was identified there as Lt. (A/Capt) R. C. Longley, London Regiment.

Gunner William Charles Longley of the Royal Marine Artillery died at the age of 24 in an accident on board HMS Collingwood on 7 March 1918. I chanced upon his grave in the Lyness Naval Cemetery on the island of Hoy in the Orkneys. So far as I know we are not related.

Eight of the poems appeared in limited editions: six in *The Lake without a Name*, with wood engravings by Jeffrey Morgan (Blackstaff Press, 2006) and two in *The Rope-makers*, with a frontispiece by Sarah Longley (Enitharmon Press, 2005).

I wish to thank the Trustees of the Ireland Chair of Poetry for appointing me to the Professorship for three very rewarding years, 2008–2010.

Some of these poems have appeared previously in *Acumen*, *Agenda*, *Akzente*, *American Scholar*, *An Sionnach*, *Aquarius*, *Archipelago*, *Best of Irish Poetry 2010*, *Colby Quarterly*, *Five Points*, *Guardian*, *Irish Pages*, *Irish Times*, *London Review of Books*, *Metre*, *New Yorker*, *Poetry Review*, *Poetry Ireland Review*, *The Shop*, *Times Literary Supplement*, *Weber: The Contemporary West*; and on RTE and BBC.

meadowsweet
loosestrife
swaying along
the ditch
waiting to
cross over
at the end
of my days